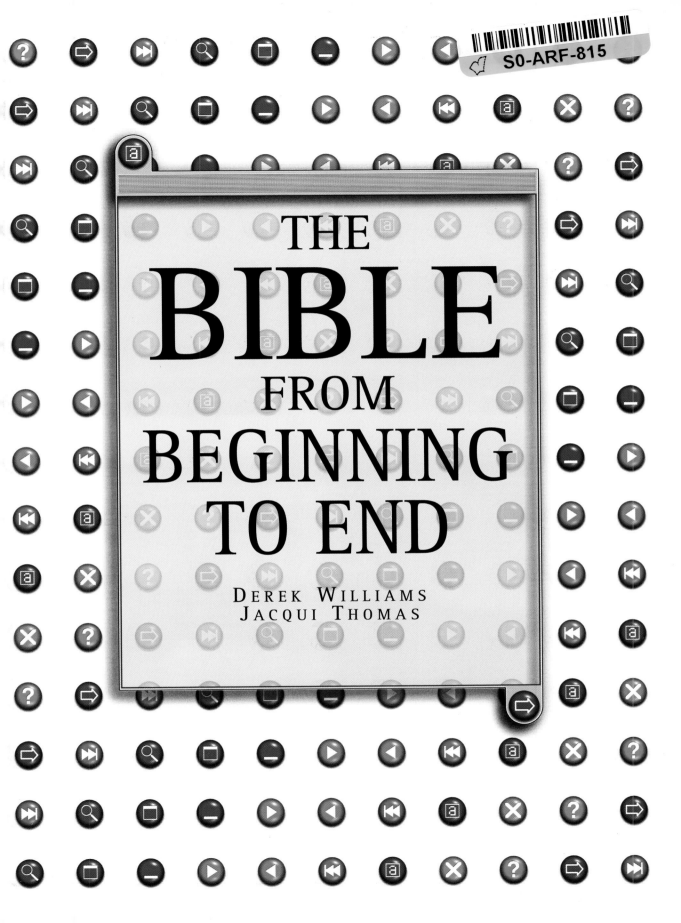

THE
BIBLE
FROM
BEGINNING
TO END

DEREK WILLIAMS
JACQUI THOMAS

CONTENTS

GOD'S WONDERFUL WORLD

There was a time when the world did not exist. But God did. God decided to make the universe so that there would be creatures God could share love with. Just by looking at it, people would learn what God was like. It was beautiful, because God was wonderful and full of love. It was perfect and majestic. So was God...

EDEN
The exact location of the Garden of Eden is unknown. Two of the rivers the Bible mentions, the Tigris and Euphrates, can be found in Mesopotamia (northern Iraq or southern Turkey). Archaeologists have found traces of the very earliest civilisations there.

CREATION
The Bible tells us that God made the world carefully. It was not an accident. The Bible says God made the world in six days.

GOD MADE...

God made the world step by step: light and dark, clouds and sky, seas and dry land. God made trees and plants to grow on the land, fish to swim in the sea and birds to fly in the air. Then God made lots of different animals, from ants to zebras. But none of them could talk to God.

ADAM AND EVE

God made people. Like the animals they had bodies that needed food. But they were also like God; they could think for themselves and they could talk to God. God put two people called Adam and Eve in a garden called Eden. God told them to look after it and to name the animals. So they set to work...

Adam and Eve named all the animals.

WORK AND REST

God rested on the seventh day and this example was followed by the humans God created; they could worship God and rest. God told Adam and Eve that they could eat the fruit from all the trees in the garden except "the tree of the knowledge of good and evil". The trouble was...

First Eve, then Adam, ate the fruit from the forbidden tree.

FALL

First Eve, and then Adam, ate the fruit from the forbidden tree. They didn't drop dead, but they felt awful. They knew they had done something wrong and that nothing could change it. They tried to hide from God, but God made them tell the truth. God was angry and sad, because nothing bad could live in God's perfect world. Adam and Eve had to leave it.

TEMPTATION

It looked so good. God had said they would die if they touched the fruit. But they didn't know what that meant. Then into the garden came an enemy of God, a cunning and evil angel called Satan. He hated God and wanted to spoil everything. He appeared to them as a snake. "Did God really say you mustn't eat from that tree?" he asked. "You won't die. Try it."

Adam and Eve were sent away from the Garden of Eden.

THE FALL

Adam and Eve's sin is sometimes called "the fall" because people fell from perfect obedience to God and chose to ignore God's laws. As a result, the Bible says that everyone is born wanting to please themselves rather than God. That is how pain and suffering started.

AMAZING FACTS

Did you know that a slug has 27,000 teeth? Or that the human body has 10 trillion (10 million million) cells? Or that there are 200,000 times more nerve connections between cells in an adult's brain than there are people on the whole earth? God made an amazing world!

The snake tempted Eve to disobey God.

THE TREE

No one knows what the "tree of knowledge" was. Paintings often show it as an apple tree, but the Bible does not say what it was. It may have been an ordinary tree which God made special. Perhaps it was meant to show people that there have to be rules in life.

1000 BC   750 BC   500 BC   250 BC   BC/AD

THE GREAT FLOOD

Adam and Eve missed being close to God, but God still loved them. They had two sons, Cain and Abel. One day these two young men took gifts to offer to God: Abel took his best sheep, and Cain took some fruit. God wasn't happy with Cain's offering, perhaps because God knew that Cain did not really worship God. When Cain killed Abel in anger and jealousy, crime entered the world...

The ark looked like a floating box rather than a boat.

FLOOD STORIES

People of other cultures also had stories about floods. Some of them have a similar theme to the Bible story. The point of the story of Noah is that the flood destroyed a world of people who were selfish and violent.

A BAD WORLD

As the years went by, people forgot about God and things got worse. People just did what they liked and ignored God's rules. Stealing and even killing were everyday happenings.

God was sad that the people God had made were disobedient. So God made a plan to start again.

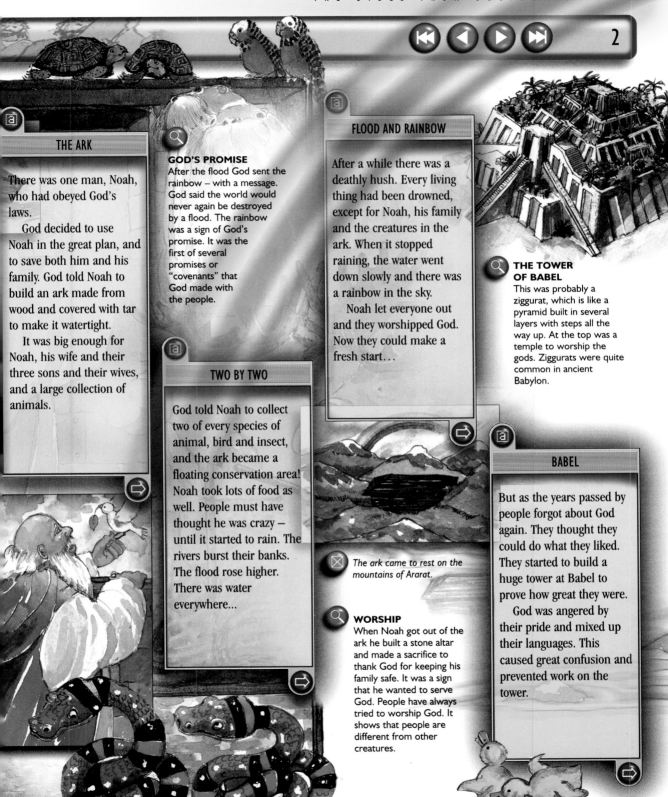

THE ARK

There was one man, Noah, who had obeyed God's laws.

God decided to use Noah in the great plan, and to save both him and his family. God told Noah to build an ark made from wood and covered with tar to make it watertight.

It was big enough for Noah, his wife and their three sons and their wives, and a large collection of animals.

GOD'S PROMISE

After the flood God sent the rainbow – with a message. God said the world would never again be destroyed by a flood. The rainbow was a sign of God's promise. It was the first of several promises or "covenants" that God made with the people.

TWO BY TWO

God told Noah to collect two of every species of animal, bird and insect, and the ark became a floating conservation area! Noah took lots of food as well. People must have thought he was crazy – until it started to rain. The rivers burst their banks. The flood rose higher. There was water everywhere...

FLOOD AND RAINBOW

After a while there was a deathly hush. Every living thing had been drowned, except for Noah, his family and the creatures in the ark. When it stopped raining, the water went down slowly and there was a rainbow in the sky.

Noah let everyone out and they worshipped God. Now they could make a fresh start…

The ark came to rest on the mountains of Ararat.

WORSHIP

When Noah got out of the ark he built a stone altar and made a sacrifice to thank God for keeping his family safe. It was a sign that he wanted to serve God. People have always tried to worship God. It shows that people are different from other creatures.

THE TOWER OF BABEL

This was probably a ziggurat, which is like a pyramid built in several layers with steps all the way up. At the top was a temple to worship the gods. Ziggurats were quite common in ancient Babylon.

BABEL

But as the years passed by people forgot about God again. They thought they could do what they liked. They started to build a huge tower at Babel to prove how great they were.

God was angered by their pride and mixed up their languages. This caused great confusion and prevented work on the tower.

1000 BC   750 BC   500 BC   250 BC

ABRAHAM'S JOURNEY

Abraham, like Noah, was a man who took God seriously. Originally from Ur in Babylonia, his family moved west to Haran where Abraham heard God telling him to go further south into Canaan. God also told him that he would have more descendants than he could count, and that they would live in that land. But Abraham and his wife, Sarah, had no children…

THE JOURNEY

Abraham's journey was across the "fertile crescent" in northern Mesopotamia where there was plenty of water and food. People lived in tents and traveled with their entire household, including servants and flocks. Archaeologists say that many people were on the move at this time.

SODOM AND GOMORRAH

These were cities near the Dead Sea. Hot tar and ash poured over the cities and destroyed them. Lot's wife stopped to look back and was buried alive by the ash and salt as it rained down.

ISAAC IS BORN

When everything seemed hopeless, Abraham and Sarah had a baby. It was a miracle! He was called Isaac. God's promise had come true. But Sarah was jealous of Hagar, the mother of Ishmael, and sent them away. God took pity on them and promised that Ishmael would start another great people.

GOD'S PROMISE

Abraham was puzzled. God had promised him a son, but now he and Sarah were too old to have children. He trusted God – but nothing had happened. So Abraham took a second wife, Hagar, who had a son called Ishmael. Abraham was pleased, but God told him to wait for the son he would have with his wife Sarah.

LOT'S ESCAPE

Meanwhile trouble was brewing. Abraham's nephew Lot lived in Sodom, where the people were very bad. God decided to destroy the cities of Sodom and Gomorrah. Abraham prayed that God would spare Lot, so an angel rescued Lot and his family just before hot ash buried the city.

HAGAR

Hagar was the servant of Sarah and the mother of Abraham's son, Ishmael. She was sent away and wandered in the desert of Beersheba.

ABRAHAM'S FAITH

Abraham was an amazing man. He waited a very long time for God to fulfil the promise of a son. The Bible says that Abraham trusted, or believed, God. He did the same when he was asked to sacrifice Isaac. The New Testament says this is an example of how everyone should trust God.

GOD'S PEOPLE

Abraham's story is the beginning of the story of God's people. The early chapters of Genesis introduce the great themes of who God is, what God wants, and why there are bad things in the world. From this point, we read about how God called a special group of people to love and serve God.

JACOB AND ESAU

Abraham's twin grandsons, Esau and Jacob, were very different. Esau loved hunting; Jacob liked cooking and staying at home.

Esau sold his birthright for some lentil stew.

ON MOUNT MORIAH

One day, when Isaac was twelve, Abraham heard God calling him to offer Isaac as a sacrifice! It was strange – sacrifices were usually animals, but Abraham set off with Isaac for Mount Moriah. Right at the last minute, as Abraham got ready to kill his son, God gave him an alternative sacrifice – a ram. God was pleased with Abraham's faith.

HUMAN SACRIFICE

Later in the Old Testament, God's law did not allow people to sacrifice human beings. But people of other tribes did. The Bible makes it clear that God did not intend Abraham to kill Isaac. God used it as a way to test and strengthen Abraham's faith.

JACOB AND ESAU

When Isaac grew up, he married Rebekah and they had twin boys, Jacob and Esau. They were always fighting. Esau was his father's favorite, Jacob was his mother's favorite. The eldest son had certain special rights but Jacob cheated Esau of these in a clever trick. Fearing for his life after the deception, he ran...

DREAMS COME TRUE

As Isaac lay dying, he called for Esau, his eldest son and his favorite, so he could bless him with a special blessing. But his wife Rebekah got her second son, Jacob, to dress up like Esau and get the blessing for himself. When Esau found out, he was furious. He threatened to kill Jacob, who fled to his uncle's farm. On the way, all alone, Jacob dreamt of angels from heaven, and he heard God promise to look after him.

FAVORITE SON

Jacob had twelve sons and one daughter. Foolishly, he had a favorite son – Joseph. Jacob gave him a special, expensive coat. Not surprisingly, his older brothers were jealous.

When Joseph dreamt that his brothers would bow before him, they decided to get rid of him…

JACOB'S WIVES

Far from home, Jacob worked for his uncle Laban and married his daughters, Leah and Rachel.

Years later he went back to Canaan. On the way, he met a stranger who injured him in a fight. Was this man an angel? Or was it God? Whichever was true, Jacob realised he had to stop fighting and start trusting God.

When he finally met Esau, his brother forgave him.

JACOB'S SHEEP
As a young man, Jacob helped his uncle Laban look after his flocks of sheep, agreeing to take the speckled sheep as his wages. Laban thought it was a good deal because there weren't many speckled sheep. But Jacob learned how to breed them and he became rich. Speckled sheep are still called "Jacob's sheep" today.

Esau forgave Jacob.

Jacob gave Joseph a special coat. This made the brothers jealous.

DREAMS
God gave Joseph the ability to interpret dreams. God can use dreams to speak to people, but it does not mean that all dreams are messages from God.

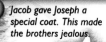

1800–1300 BC   1250 BC

Slaves were treated harshly in Egypt.

EGYPT

Egypt is south and west of Canaan. It is hot and dry but along the River Nile the ground is rich and fertile. It was a strong country in Old Testament times: sometimes it helped the nation of Israel and sometimes it controlled them.

ISRAEL IN EGYPT

Jacob was the father of twelve sons, founders of the tribes of Israel. Joseph and his descendants stayed in Egypt for 400 years and became a large group of people. Then another pharaoh made them all slaves, as Joseph had once been, and they were in trouble.

FOOD IN EGYPT

Later, when food was short, Joseph's brothers came from Canaan to buy grain! Joseph's dream had come true: they bowed down before him. At first they didn't recognise him. When he was sure they were sorry for their actions, he told them who he was and all that had happened to him. Then the whole family came to live in Egypt.

SUCCESS FOR JOSEPH

In prison, Joseph interpreted the dreams of two prisoners. Then the pharaoh started dreaming. No one could tell him what his dreams meant until someone remembered Joseph. Joseph said the dreams predicted seven good harvests and seven bad ones.

"Store food now," he advised.

The pharaoh was so pleased with Joseph's advice that he put Joseph in charge of the stores.

JOSEPH IN PRISON

Some slave traders came by.

"Let's make some money!" the brothers said.

They sold Joseph as a slave and told their father he had been killed by a wild animal. Joseph was taken to Egypt where he worked for an army officer, Potiphar. But Potiphar's wife told lies about him and had Joseph thrown into prison…

Joseph's brothers came to Egypt to beg for food.

ESCAPE TO FREEDOM

Every day it was the same. Shouting slave drivers cracking their whips. The Israelites were forced to work all day at the brick fields and building sites. They were slaves in Egypt, and they hated it. But God had a plan for their rescue, and it involved a shepherd called Moses...

THE NILE
The River Nile was the main source of water for both people and animals. The Egyptians dug canals from the river to water their fields of crops. If anything happened to the Nile, the Egyptians would starve.

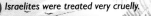
Israelites were treated very cruelly.

BABY IN THE BASKET
Moses had been born in Egypt, the son of Israelite slaves. His mother hid him in a basket on the River Nile when the pharaoh ordered all Israelite baby boys to be killed. He was found by the pharaoh's daughter, who adopted him and brought him up as her son.

MOSES THE MURDERER
When Moses grew up, he saw an Egyptian beating an Israelite slave. He was so enraged that he killed the Egyptian and fled to Midian where he became a shepherd.

Moses saw a bush on fire but not burning up.

BURNING BUSH

Moses could not believe his eyes! He saw a bush on fire but not burning up. Then he heard God speaking.

"Lead my people out of slavery," God said.

"I can't," replied Moses. "They'll never believe me. And I'm no good at speaking."

God promised to help Moses through miracles, and Aaron, Moses' brother, could do the talking. So they went to see the pharaoh...

PLAGUES

Moses pleaded with the pharaoh.

"Let my people go!" he said.

But the pharaoh made the Israelite slaves work even harder. Then God struck Egypt with nine terrible plagues: water pollution, frogs, gnats, flies, animal disease, human sores, hail, locusts and darkness.

Still the king said no. Until one day...

PRE-HISTORY	2000 BC	1750 BC	1500 BC	1250 BC

Locusts ate all the crops.

THE TEN PLAGUES OF EGYPT

There were ten plagues in all. First the River Nile was turned into blood. Then there were plagues of frogs, gnats and flies. The fifth plague killed cattle, and the sixth gave boils to both animals and people. The seventh plague was of terrible hail, and the eighth brought locusts that devoured everything. The ninth brought darkness and the tenth killed all of the Egyptians' firstborn sons.

PASSOVER MEAL

On the final night before the Israelites left the land of Egypt, they dressed as if for a journey and ate a meal of roast lamb and herbs and unleavened bread. This meal was forever afterwards known as the Passover meal, for the angel of the Lord passed over the houses where the Israelites were, ready to leave. The tenth plague struck only the households of the Egyptians.

DEATH

God caused the eldest son in every Egyptian family to die.

The Israelites were safe from this plague, as they had been from all the others. They had a special meal (the Passover), put a sign on their doors to show they trusted God and packed their bags.

The next day, the Egyptians could not wait to get rid of the Israelites. They had had enough of them and begged them to leave. They even gave them golden jewellery to get rid of them. So the Israelites ran...

The pharaoh told the Israelites to go.

EXODUS

The *exodus* is the name given to this event, when the Israelites left the slavery of the Egyptians and crossed the Red Sea. The word *exodus* means "going out". This event marked the beginning of the Israelite nation.

DRY PATH

... straight towards the marshes near the Red Sea. They carried all their belongings, and drove their sheep and goats across the countryside.

However, Pharaoh changed his mind and sent his army after them. The Israelites arrived at the marshes.

"They're cornered!" cried the pharaoh.

But Moses said God would save them. As Moses stretched out his stick, a wind blew a dry path across the marshes. The Israelites hurried across to safety.

Then, as the Egyptians arrived, Moses dropped his arm, the wind stopped, the water flowed back, and the Israelites were safe.

LOST IN THE DESERT

Free at last! Led by Moses, the Israelites left Egypt and headed north to Canaan, the land God had promised them. The quick way up the coast was too dangerous – the Philistines were on the warpath. So God's people went the long way, southwards into the Arabian desert. In the desert there was no food or water, and there were no towns or cities where they could buy supplies...

GOD LEADS

The people learned to obey God. God led them by a pillar of cloud by day and a pillar of fire by night. One day Moses went up Mount Sinai. It was awesome; the people could feel God's presence. God gave Moses Ten Commandments which summed up the way to live. But Moses was away so long that the people thought he had died.

God gave the Israelites water from a rock.

The Ten Commandments.

GOD PROVIDES FOOD

The Israelites had to trust God. God showed Moses where to get water and it burst out of a rock when Moses prayed. Then God sent "manna" each day and when they asked for meat, God sent a flock of quail which they were able to catch.

FOOD IN THE DESERT
God sent special food called manna which fell from the sky each night. It was white, fluffy and delicious. It did not stay fresh, so the Israelites had to rely on God each day. Quails are birds the size of small chickens. They migrate across the Arabian desert, but sometimes fall to the ground exhausted.

PRE-HISTORY   2000 BC   1750 BC   1500 BC   1250 BC

THE TEN COMMANDMENTS

These laws sum up the way God wants people everywhere to live: they tell people to worship only the one true God, to rest from work one day a week, to respect their parents, to be faithful in their marriages and not to murder, steal or tell lies.

MOUNT SINAI

Also called Mount Horeb in the Bible, no one knows today quite where it was. At the top of the mountain, in clouds and thunder and lightning, Moses met God and received the Ten Commandments, written on two large stones.

THE GOLDEN CALF

The people said they wanted to worship something, so Aaron (Moses' brother) made a calf out of gold. Just as they began to worship it, Moses arrived with the commandments. He was furious as they had broken God's first two laws already!

God started to punish them, but Moses pleaded with God to stop before they all died.

THE TENT OF MEETING

The Israelites built a portable tent called the tent of meeting as a center for worshipping God. The tent had two rooms. The Holy Place had a lampstand and a table. The Most Holy Place housed the sacred chest (Ark of the Covenant), which held the Ten Commandments and symbolised God's presence.

SPIES IN CANAAN

One day, Moses sent twelve spies into Canaan, the land God had promised them. They came back amazed.

"It's a great place!" they said. "But the people living there are too strong for us."

Two of the spies, Joshua and Caleb disagreed. "God will help us," they insisted.

But no one believed them. So God said that no one would go there except Joshua and Caleb.

FORTY YEARS

Despite being so close, the Israelites spent many more years in the desert.

They moaned and grumbled about the food and about Moses. Even Moses' own sister rebelled against him. Then some men led by Korah rebelled – and the earth swallowed them up.

But the Israelites did follow God's instructions and built the tent of meeting, the center of their life together, where they could worship God.

A FERTILE LAND

The spies who returned from Canaan brought back grapes, figs and pomegranates to show what a wonderful, rich place it was.

HOME AT LAST!

It was forty years since the Israelites left Egypt.
Moses was dead and his successor, Joshua, was to
lead the people into Canaan, the land God had
promised them. It was just across the River Jordan.
Joshua was faced with two problems;
this land was settled by other people and
the river was in flood.

Rahab hid the spies.

CROSSING THE JORDAN

The Israelites had come up
the east side of the Dead
Sea and had to cross the
river into Canaan.

Normally it was quite
shallow, but it was
springtime and the river
was swollen by rain.

Joshua prayed to God
and the water stopped
flowing. The river had
become blocked upstream,
so the people crossed on
dry land.

SAFETY FOR RAHAB

Before they crossed over
the River Jordan, Joshua
sent spies into Jericho.
They stayed at the house
of a woman called Rahab,
who hid them under some
flax drying on the roof. The
spies promised that Rahab
and her family would be
saved when they invaded
the city.

JOSHUA:
A GODLY LEADER

Joshua had been Moses'
assistant while the
Israelites were in the
desert. He had been one
of the spies who had
believed God would give
Canaan to the Israelites.
God had told Joshua to
listen and be obedient to
God, which he did, and to
be strong and courageous,
because God would be
with him.

JERICHO

Archaeologists have found
evidence of habitation in
this oasis city dating back
to 8000 BC. At one time it
was a large fortified city
with walls so thick that
houses were built into it.

The Israelites crossed the river on dry land.

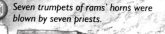

Seven trumpets of rams' horns were blown by seven priests.

A NEW LAND

Then the battles started again. Eventually, with God's help the Israelites controlled much of the land.

Joshua divided it up between the twelve tribes and sent them to make new lives and homes. He appointed judges to sort out any problems and they dedicated themselves to God yet again.

THE TWELVE TRIBES

Descended from Jacob's sons, each tribe had its own area to live in, except for the tribe of Levi. The Levites were to look after the religious worship, so they were given towns in each tribal area. Two other tribes were descended from Joseph's sons, Ephraim and Manasseh.

THE BATTLE OF JERICHO

Once the Israelites had crossed the river they stopped to worship God, set up a monument to remind future generations of what God had done and dedicated themselves to God once more.

Then they arrived at Jericho for their first battle where they were told to march in silence round the city once a day for six days!

The seventh day they marched seven times. The priests blew on their trumpets, the people shouted loudly and the walls fell down.

GOD'S BATTLE

Joshua told the Israelites that God had won the battle for them, but one person ruined everything.

God had told the Israelites to destroy all the things they found in Jericho, but Achan rather liked them. He hid his booty in his tent.

When the Israelites went to their next battle at Ai, they lost. God said it was because someone had been disobedient. They found out it was Achan, and he was punished.

TOTAL DESTRUCTION

The invading Israelites were told to destroy everything and everyone they found. It stopped defeated peoples from recovering and hitting back. The Israelites were told they could keep nothing, as a sign that they were God's people and were called to be different from other nations.

1000 BC   750 BC   500 BC

Achan hid "booty" in his tent.

HEROES TO THE RESCUE!

Joshua had helped the Israelites settle into Canaan, but when he died, there was nobody to succeed him. Instead, there were judges in each tribe who sorted out arguments. Soon though, the people forgot God's law. They turned to other gods. Then other tribes attacked the Israelites, which was God's way of showing they had done wrong. When they cried to God for help, God answered...

GIDEON

... until the Israelites did wrong again. This time, the Midianites invaded, and stole Israelite crops and animals.

The next hero was an ordinary farmer called Gideon.

One day an angel told him to save Israel. Gideon didn't care for the idea, so he asked for a sign that he had heard the message correctly: dew on the ground and not on his fleece one night, and the opposite the next. He got the sign, so he had to fight...

DEBORAH

God sent Deborah. She didn't fight, but she passed on God's orders.

The Canaanites had many chariots, and Israel didn't – so when they attacked, they just rode over Israel. Deborah told the soldier Barak to fight them, but he was terrified and asked her to go with him.

She did, and the Canaanites were beaten. There was peace for a while...

WOMEN LEADERS

Deborah was an unusual hero because there were not many women leaders at this time. Another woman who performed a heroic deed was Jael. She killed a Canaanite king as he ran away from the battle. The king stopped at Jael's tent to rest, because her husband was his ally, and she killed him with a tent peg while he was asleep. It rather put the men to shame.

WARFARE

The enemies of the Israelites rode chariots – small, fast carts pulled by horses. A couple of soldiers in each one could drive the horses and fire arrows or throw spears. They were hard targets to hit. The Israelites did not use chariots, partly because they lived in the hilly country where chariots were less useful. It may also have been because God wanted the Israelites to rely on God, and not on their weapons. The Israelite foot soldiers carried spears, arrows and swords.

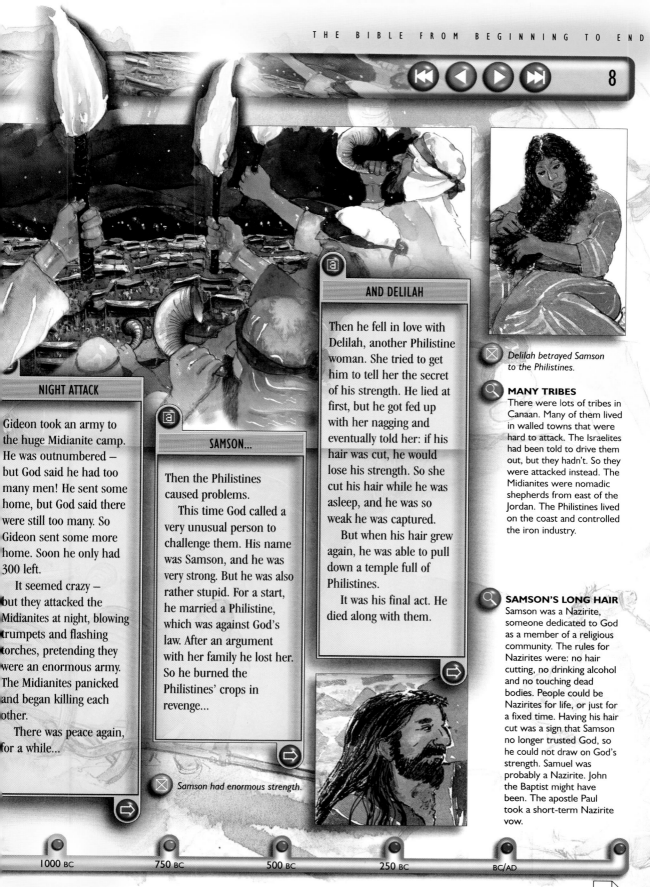

NIGHT ATTACK

Gideon took an army to the huge Midianite camp. He was outnumbered – but God said he had too many men! He sent some home, but God said there were still too many. So Gideon sent some more home. Soon he only had 300 left.

It seemed crazy – but they attacked the Midianites at night, blowing trumpets and flashing torches, pretending they were an enormous army. The Midianites panicked and began killing each other.

There was peace again, for a while...

SAMSON...

Then the Philistines caused problems.

This time God called a very unusual person to challenge them. His name was Samson, and he was very strong. But he was also rather stupid. For a start, he married a Philistine, which was against God's law. After an argument with her family he lost her. So he burned the Philistines' crops in revenge...

Samson had enormous strength.

AND DELILAH

Then he fell in love with Delilah, another Philistine woman. She tried to get him to tell her the secret of his strength. He lied at first, but he got fed up with her nagging and eventually told her: if his hair was cut, he would lose his strength. So she cut his hair while he was asleep, and he was so weak he was captured.

But when his hair grew again, he was able to pull down a temple full of Philistines.

It was his final act. He died along with them.

Delilah betrayed Samson to the Philistines.

MANY TRIBES

There were lots of tribes in Canaan. Many of them lived in walled towns that were hard to attack. The Israelites had been told to drive them out, but they hadn't. So they were attacked instead. The Midianites were nomadic shepherds from east of the Jordan. The Philistines lived on the coast and controlled the iron industry.

SAMSON'S LONG HAIR

Samson was a Nazirite, someone dedicated to God as a member of a religious community. The rules for Nazirites were: no hair cutting, no drinking alcohol and no touching dead bodies. People could be Nazirites for life, or just for a fixed time. Having his hair cut was a sign that Samson no longer trusted God, so he could not draw on God's strength. Samuel was probably a Nazirite. John the Baptist might have been. The apostle Paul took a short-term Nazirite vow.

A KING FOR ISRAEL

For many years in Israel, the leaders called "judges" came and went. Time and again the Israelites turned back to God, but then forget God again. There was an old priest in Shiloh called Eli. He loved God, but his sons were selfish and greedy. So God sent a young boy there, who became the last and greatest of the judges, and the first of the great prophets.

SAMUEL THE JUDGE

The Bible focuses mostly on the big events in Samuel's life. But most of the time Samuel's leadership of Israel as a "judge" was similar to a modern judge. He traveled around a "circuit" – a number of towns in turn – to sort out disputes between people. He was also a priest, so he led them in worship too.

GOD SPEAKS

Hannah had prayed for years to have a son. Eventually, God answered her prayers and Samuel was born.

Hannah dedicated him to God and he grew up as Eli's helper at Shiloh.

One night, when Samuel was still quite young, God spoke to him. Samuel was amazed, but the message he had to give was not an easy one. God said the Israelites would be punished because they had disobeyed God's laws.

SAMUEL

Samuel grew up to be a good, wise, and holy man.

When the Philistines captured the sacred chest (Ark of the Covenant), it seemed as if God had left the Israelites. But the Philistines sent it back and Samuel called the Israelites to love God again. They said they would, and Samuel became their leader. But when Samuel got old...

THE CALL OF SAMUEL

When Samuel was awakened by a voice calling him in the night, he thought it was Eli, the priest. But when God called him for the third time, Eli realised that the voice Samuel heard was God's. He told him to reply, "Speak Lord, your servant is listening."

WE WANT A KING!

The tribal leaders asked Samuel to appoint a king. Samuel was horrified – didn't they know that God was their king? He warned them that a human king would have complete power over people, and would make them pay heavy taxes. He might even turn the people into slaves

However the Israelites insisted, so God showed Samuel what to do.

SHILOH

This was a town in central Israel where the tent of meeting was placed for many years, making it an important center where people came to worship God and offer sacrifices. It was destroyed by the Philistines during Saul's lifetime.

The sacred chest (Ark of the Covenant)

Samuel anointed
Saul king.

SAUL IS KING

God led Samuel to a young
man called Saul. At a great
feast for all Israel, Saul
was made king. At first,
everyone liked him and he
won many battles.
Unfortunately, then he
started to disobey God. He
offered sacrifices, which
was not his job.

It was then the Philistine
Goliath challenged Israel's
champion fighters to a
duel.

SAUL
He was tall, good-looking
and very able. But he had
little faith in God. After
Samuel had died, he tried
to get in touch with the
prophet by going to a
spiritualist medium, which
was forbidden. He became
mentally unstable too, and
tried to kill David several
times. He died in battle.

GOLIATH
He was an
unusually tall and
strong man. It was the
custom in ancient times for
disputes between nations
to be settled by a contest
between the champion
fighters of both sides.
Whoever won the duel
was said to have won the
war.

David killed Goliath with
a stone from his sling.

DAVID AND GOLIATH

Goliath was huge and no
one had the courage to
fight him, except a young
boy called David. He just
went out and used a
simple shepherd's sling
and a stone to kill him.

Everyone was delighted,
except for Saul. He began
to realise that David could
become a rival. He was
right, as in God's plan,
David was to be the next
king.

THE PHILISTINES
They were the people who gave Palestine (the area which
includes Israel) its name. They probably originated in Crete
and they lived near the coast. They controlled the iron
industry so the Israelites had to go to them for tools and
weapons. Eventually, David defeated them.

1050 BC   750 BC   500 BC   250 BC   BC/AD

DAVID THE GODLY LEADER

While Saul was still king, God told Samuel secretly to give his blessing to David, a shepherd boy, to take over the throne after Saul died. For many years David was on the run as Saul tried to kill him, but David always refused to kill Saul when he had the chance. After Saul's death, there was civil war for a while until everyone agreed that David should be king.

DAVID THE SOLDIER

David wanted to build a Temple for God in Jerusalem.

But Nathan the prophet told him that while the idea pleased God, David wasn't the right person to do it. He was a soldier, spending his life defending and rescuing Israel from its enemies; a Temple should be built by a peaceful king.

David made plans so his son could build it.

MUSIC AND POETRY
David wrote some of the Psalms in the Bible. The words were written down but the music was not. Tunes probably sounded like medieval chants. The poetry does not rhyme, or scan for a rhythm. Instead, it plays with ideas, looking at the same thing different ways, using picture-language.

DAVID
The youngest of eight sons of Jesse who lived in Bethlehem, David was a shepherd boy who learned to use his sling to fend off wild animals. He also played the harp and wrote poetry.

CAPITAL CITY

First David captured Jerusalem, a hilltop fortress held by the Jebusites. They thought they were safe inside, but David knew of a secret water tunnel. He led his men through it and surprised everyone.

Jerusalem became David's capital city, and he brought the sacred chest (Ark of the Covenant) there to show that it was God's city.

There was dancing in the streets as the people celebrated and worshipped God.

SHEPHERDS AND SLINGS
In David's time, shepherds had a hard life. They camped out in the fields and had to protect their flocks against bears, wolves and even lions. The sling carried by shepherds was a band of fabric or leather. The stone was placed in the middle. The slinger held both ends, swung it round his head fast, then let go of one end so the stone would fly out at great speed.

DAVID
THE MODEL KING

From this point on, the Bible looks forward to a new king who would be like David and would be descended from David's family. He would be a man of God to start a new era of peace and prosperity. Christians believe that Jesus was this savior; he came from David's family, too.

DAVID'S DOWNFALL

Slowly David drove back the enemy tribes in Israel. But as he grew older, David got tired of war and sent the army out without him.

Foolishly, he took Bathsheba, who was already married, to be his wife, and had her husband killed in a battle.

He was devastated when he realised how he had broken God's laws, and so he turned back to God, but then even his own children turned against him.

FAMILY FEUD

There was a feud between two of David's sons: Amnon attacked his half-sister Tamar, and so Absalom killed Amnon. Then Absalom tried to make himself king by raising an army and forcing David to leave Jerusalem. Joab, David's commander, killed Absalom — even though David had said his son should be captured alive. David was full of grief at his son's death.

DAVID DIES

When David knew he was dying, he sent for Solomon, the son born to Bathsheba. He reminded his son to be obedient to God so that God would bless his descendants on the throne of Israel.

David had ruled for forty years. He had made some bad mistakes, but he knew God's forgiveness. He loved God and wanted others to love God too.

When he died, Israel was a wealthy country, and its enemies had been defeated.

DEATH OF ABSALOM
Joab plunged three javelins into Absalom's chest while he hung from the branches of an oak tree.

JERUSALEM
This hilltop city (also called "Zion" in the Bible) became the capital of Israel. It was small in David's time, but today is a large city. It has been attacked many times. The Bible records its destruction by the Babylonians in 587 BC and predicted its destruction by the Romans in AD 70.

SOLOMON'S WEALTH AND WISDOM

The next king after David was Solomon. David had made sure that Israel was at peace and no one dared attack. So Solomon spent his time and money on doing good things. He made trade agreements with many countries and all Israel became very rich. Most important of all, Solomon was wise and he trusted God...

WISDOM
Wisdom in the Bible means understanding God's will and doing what is right in every situation. The Book of Proverbs is full of common sense advice such as "work hard", "keep secrets" and "don't be friends with bad people". These are practical ways of living as God wants us to.

THE TEMPLE
The Temple was divided into three sections inside. The first was a porch that led into the Holy Place where there were tables for the sacred bread, an altar of incense and lampstands. That led into the Most Holy Place, where the sacred chest (Ark of the Covenant) was kept. Only the high priest could go in there. All the animal sacrifices were made at an altar outside. There was a large basin outside, too, where the priests washed everything.

Priests washed at the basin outside the Temple.

WISE SOLOMON

Everyone dreams of having their greatest wish come true. But it really happened to Solomon. One night God told him to ask for whatever he wanted. But instead of asking for fame or riches, Solomon asked for wisdom to rule God's people. He knew he had a hard job ahead and he couldn't do it well without God's help.

God was pleased; it showed Solomon wasn't greedy. So God made him rich as well...

WHOSE BABY?

He needed God's wisdom, though. One day, two women brought a problem to him. They both claimed to be the mother of a baby and that the other woman's baby had died. Solomon thought for a minute, then said the simplest answer was to cut the baby in half! One woman agreed, but the other was horrified and wanted her rival to have the baby rather than see her baby die.

Solomon knew that she was the real mother. He gave it back to her – uncut! – and his fame spread...

GOD'S TEMPLE

"If you want to be wise, trust God" Solomon said (Proverbs 1:7).

He practiced what he preached. He put God first, and wanted others to as well. So he ordered the Temple to be built in Jerusalem.

It took seven years. It was panelled with cedar wood inside with lots of gold decoration. He hired the best craftsmen and bought the finest materials. When it was finished, everyone felt God's presence there.

WORSHIP
The Israelites were required to attend the Temple three times a year for the Passover, Pentecost and Tabernacles festivals. At other times, they observed feasts locally, but all sacrifices were supposed to be made in Jerusalem. In practice, they didn't do this very often. All through Old Testament times, people tried to worship other gods as well as the Lord. Even though they had been taught that there was only one God, they carried on following after false gods.

SACRIFICES
Most tribes sacrificed animals at this time in history. God gave the Israelites a special message in their sacrifices, though. They show how seriously God takes doing wrong. But God is kind, and wants people to know God. So the sacrifices also showed that God would forgive people if something else took the punishment for their sins.

QUEEN OF SHEBA

People came from far away to hear Solomon's wisdom and see his wealth. One visitor was the queen of Sheba, who brought him gifts.

Solomon collected wise sayings, and some are included in the Bible's Book of Proverbs.

For example: "Laziness makes a man poor; hard work makes a man rich" (Proverbs 10:4); "A fool is right in his own eyes but a wise man listens to advice" (Proverbs 12:15).

OTHER GODS

Solomon sealed his trade deals with other nations by marrying the daughters of the kings he traded with. (It was the custom to have many wives.) Solomon let these women bring their own gods and priests with them, and the Israelites started to worship these idols. Because of this, God brought tribes to attack Israel.

ROYAL TRADE
The queen of Sheba probably came from southern Arabia, possibly near modern Yemen. Solomon imported spices and perfumes from Arabia. They were much prized in those days, to make food tasty and people smell nice! (People got very hot and sweaty in the heat.) He also imported wood and cloth from Hiram, the king of Tyre in the north. The Tyrians were good sailors. They manned the ships Solomon used. He paid for his goods in olive oil and grain from Israel's farmlands.

THE KINGDOM FALLS APART

Solomon had given Israel a golden age of peace and prosperity. But he had paid for his many building projects (palaces, stables, stores and offices) by making the people pay lots of taxes. This didn't make them happy. When Solomon died, his son Rehoboam became king, and the people began to bargain with him.

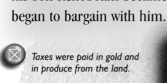

Taxes were paid in gold and in produce from the land.

BAD ADVICE

A number of leaders in Israel, including Jeroboam, came to Rehoboam and asked for fewer taxes.

"If you make the load lighter, we'll follow you," they said. Rehoboam talked to his advisers.

The older men said, "Make it lighter."

The younger men said, "Don't be soft! Get all you can!"

Rehoboam took the view of the younger men: more taxes!

THE KINGDOM SPLITS

The people rebelled: ten tribes north of Jerusalem voted to have Jeroboam as their king; only two tribes in the south wanted to follow Rehoboam, out of loyalty to Solomon's family.

The northern tribes were called *Israel* and the southern tribes *Judah*.

NORTH-SOUTH DIVIDE

The city of Dan was in the far north of the Northern Kingdom, named after the Israelite tribe of Dan. There had been a center of worship there since the time of the judges. The Land of Israel (which includes Judah) was sometimes described as "from Dan (north) to Beersheba (south)".

People went to worship at pagan shrines.

MANY GODS

In Bible times the Israelites were unusual because they believed in the one God who had made the world and everything in it, and who had a special relationship with the people. Other tribes believed there were many gods and spirits which had to be kept happy by giving them sacrifices and worship. Today some people believe in forces that are said to influence their lives, such as astrology. The Bible says that God is in control of people's lives, and that the Holy Spirit can show people the right way to live, and give them the power to do it.

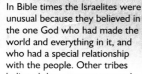

BULL STATUES
Bull calves were often used to represent gods in ancient times. They were symbols of fertility and strength. The Israelites had made a similar statue in the desert when Moses went away up Mount Sinai to receive the Ten Commandments.

OTHER GODS

In the south, Rehoboam wasn't much better. He wasn't a bit like Solomon. He didn't worship God even though the Temple was outside his palace door. He brought in other gods, and built shrines, where all sorts of terrible things went on.

Rehoboam was followed by a better king, Asa, who got rid of the shrines.

It went on like that — good kings, bad kings — for years.

BULL WORSHIP

From now on, the Bible books follow each country separately.

The first problem faced by Israel (north) was that they had no Temple, as it was in Jerusalem. So King Jeroboam set up shrines in Bethel and Dan, and made statues of bulls to represent God. Unfortunately the people started worshiping the bulls, not God.

PROPHECIES

The prophets told Jeroboam that worshipping statues was wrong. Jeroboam just laughed it off and threatened the prophets, but God made him ill and he was sorry.

Later a prophet called Ahijah said that God would destroy the northern kingdom one day because of what Jeroboam had done.

PROPHETS
From now on in the Old Testament, prophets played an important role. They were good men who obeyed God, understood God's will and taught God's truth. They called for the kings and people to come back to God and they condemned the pagan gods. They warned that God would punish the people if they strayed from his ways. Some Bible books (Isaiah, Jeremiah and Ezekiel) were written by prophets.

PAGAN SHRINES
The shrines dedicated to idols and pagan gods were sometimes called "Asherah", and were often built on hilltops because the people thought they were nearer the gods. These sacred places may have been like altars or little temples, or represented by carved poles like totem poles or small groves of trees.

930–875 BC   500 BC   250 BC   BC/AD

ELIJAH – GOD'S FIRE-RAISER!

In Israel (the northern kingdom) King Ahab married Jezebel. She was not an Israelite. She came from Sidon, where pagan gods and idols were worshipped. She brought her style of worship, her idols and her priests to Israel, and set about destroying the worship of God. Ahab didn't mind. But God did, and sent the prophet Elijah to warn him.

KING AHAB
Ahab was the son of King Omri who had bought a hill at Samaria, the capital of the northern kingdom of Israel, and built on it. Ahab built a luxury palace and a temple to Baal there. It was destroyed by the Assyrians in 722 BC.

ON THE RUN

When Elijah told King Ahab there would be a drought and famine for three years as a punishment for his disobedience, Ahab was furious and threatened to kill him.

Elijah ran far away from Israel and God looked after him. First he was fed by ravens and then he went to Sidon where a widow looked after him.

Eventually God told Elijah to go back to see Ahab. He challenged Jezebel's priests of Baal to a strange duel.

ELIJAH IN HIDING
God told Elijah to hide by the brook of Cherith near the River Jordan. He drank the water from the brook during the drought and ravens brought him bread and meat every day.

BAAL
"Baal" means "Lord" and was a general name for many pagan gods. The Baal worshipped by Jezebel was probably Baal Melkart, a storm god. It was a powerful message to the people on the top of Mount Carmel when Baal couldn't make rain to end the drought and could not send fire (lightning), but God could!

ON MOUNT CARMEL

Elijah called everyone to Mount Carmel. Both Elijah and the priests of Baal prepared sacrifices – a bull to be slaughtered on an altar. Elijah challenged the priests of Baal to pray that the sacrifice would be set alight by a miracle. The priests of Baal got no answer from their god.

But when Elijah prayed, his sacrifice caught fire. The people of Israel worshipped God, and the drought ended, but the trouble didn't...

PRE-HISTORY   2000 BC   1750 BC   1500 BC   1250 BC

DEATH THREAT

Jezebel was furious! Elijah had ordered all her priests to be killed, and she issued a death threat for Elijah. He ran south into the desert. There, God spoke to him quietly.

"You're not alone," God said. "Lots more people trust me. Go back. I have more work for you."

The contest on Mount Carmel.

ELISHA

Elijah's next job was to appoint Elisha as his successor. Elisha left his farm to help Elijah. When it was time for Elijah to die, Elisha asked to receive the same spiritual power as Elijah.

"Only if you see me go to heaven," Elijah said.

Elisha saw Elijah taken up to heaven. Then he got to work...

OLIVE OIL
The oil Elisha provided for the poor widow was made from crushed olives. It was used for cooking (and it still is) and also for oil lamps, and even as a cosmetic. It was essential to the Israelites.

A GREAT PROPHET

Elisha lived through the reigns of many kings of Israel. He did many miracles: he helped a poor widow pay all her debts with a miraculous supply of oil; he raised a dead boy to life; and he healed the Syrian commander Naaman of leprosy.

After the death of Ahab, Elisha anointed Jehu as king. When the wicked Queen Jezebel was flung out of a window to her death, and dogs licked up her blood, one of Elijah's prophecies came true.

LEPROSY
When Naaman, the Syrian commander, found he had leprosy, it meant that he had to live separately from other people, and could not do his job. In Bible times, many skin diseases were called *leprosy*. They made people "unclean", which meant they could not take part in worship and they became outcasts.

DISASTER STRIKES

After Elisha died, no one in Israel (the northern kingdom) seemed to care about God any more. The people continued to worship pagan gods and idols and they became greedy and selfish. They stopped obeying God's laws. God was very patient. God didn't want to punish them, so God sent two prophets to try to make them see sense...

 THE FALL OF ISRAEL
The Assyrians came from what is now northern Iraq. They had gradually conquered the whole of the ancient near east and finally defeated Israel. They also besieged Lachish in Judah, attacking the walls using scaling ladders and battering rams.

ISRAEL'S SINS
There were the religious sins of worshipping other gods, and there were sins to do with how people lived together in society, such as not helping poor people but taking advantage of them. Judges took bribes so that poor people couldn't get justice in the courts. Amos said that God cared for the poor, and for widows and orphans, and so God's people should care for them too.

AMOS

First, God sent Amos to Israel. He was a farmer from Judah (the southern kingdom).

Amos was shocked by what he saw. People were cruel to the weak and poor. Rich landowners bought up farms and made people homeless. Many people just lived for pleasure and making money. Life for them was just one long party, but Amos knew there was more to life than fun.

JUDGEMENT

Amos said people should be kind to each other. He warned them that God would punish them if they carried on living only for their own pleasure. Although they were expecting "the day of the Lord", when God would rule with peace and prosperity, there would be a day of judgement instead.

People didn't like his message and told him to go back home, but he stayed.

HOSEA

At about the same time, Hosea was called to be a prophet. Hosea's wife, Gomer, had three children. Then Gomer walked out on Hosea and her children.

God used Hosea's family as a picture of God's message to Israel. Gomer had deserted Hosea just as Israel had deserted God. In the same way God would still love the people and welcome them back, Hosea would love his wife and bring her back into his home.

AMOS THE FARMER
Amos was a shepherd and he also grew sycamore-figs. Figs were an important source of food and the large shrubs needed careful tending. Amos was a farmer not a professional prophet, but God called him from a normal occupation to be a special messenger.

1750 BC   1500 BC   1250 BC

Hosea bought Gomer back from the slave trader.

ANOTHER CHANCE

Hosea's wife went off with other men and even became a slave. Hosea was heartbroken because he loved her.

"That's a picture," God said. "The people of Israel have left me and worshipped false gods even though I loved them."

God told Hosea to buy Gomer back from the slave trader.

"That's what I'll do for my people," God promised. "I'll give them another chance."

ASSYRIAN CAPTIVES

The people of Israel were taken into exile in Assyria. It was the policy of the Assyrians to deport captives from their homes to prevent any trouble from them later. Then the land of Israel was resettled by foreigners.

ISRAEL DESTROYED

But Israel continued to ignore God and God's laws. In 722 BC the Assyrians overran Israel, and destroyed its capital, Samaria. They took the people off to other countries and replaced them with foreign refugees. The ten tribes were destroyed and lost for ever. Then Judah, the southern kingdom, came under attack too.

1000 BC   722 BC   500 BC   250 BC   BC/AD

FALL OF JERUSALEM

In the years that followed, the kings and people of Judah disobeyed God, worshipping false idols and breaking God's laws. It was as if they thought God would never let them be defeated; after all they had the Temple, God's house, in Jerusalem. They were wrong, as the prophets kept on pointing out.

PROPHETS

The prophet Isaiah wrote the longest book in the Bible. He was an adviser to King Hezekiah. His book contains beautiful poetic descriptions of God's greatness. God called Jeremiah when he was quite young. Jeremiah said that he didn't want to be a prophet. But God promised to give him the words and God helped Jeremiah to be strong when he was threatened.

"TRUST GOD"

Then one day, the Assyrian army marched towards Jerusalem. A loud-mouthed commander surrounded the city with his troops. He shouted that no god could defeat him. People couldn't get out or bring in food. King Hezekiah was terrified.

But Isaiah the prophet told him to trust God.

Suddenly many of the Assyrian soldiers died of a mystery illness, and Judah was safe for a while.

THE KINGS

King Ahaz was bad and let the people worship other gods. He had to pay heavy taxes to the Assyrians to stop them attacking him.

But Hezekiah, his son, was a good king. He smashed up the altars and idols, restored the worship of God and kept God's laws. As a result, Judah was able to stop paying taxes to Assyria.

For a while...

HEZEKIAH'S TUNNEL

Jerusalem, the capital of Judah, was built on a craggy hill, so it was difficult to attack, but it was also easy to surround. It had no water supply inside, so in a siege, people would die of thirst. King Hezekiah built a tunnel about 550 metres long to bring water from a spring outside the city into the Pool of Siloam inside the city. The tunnel is still there today.

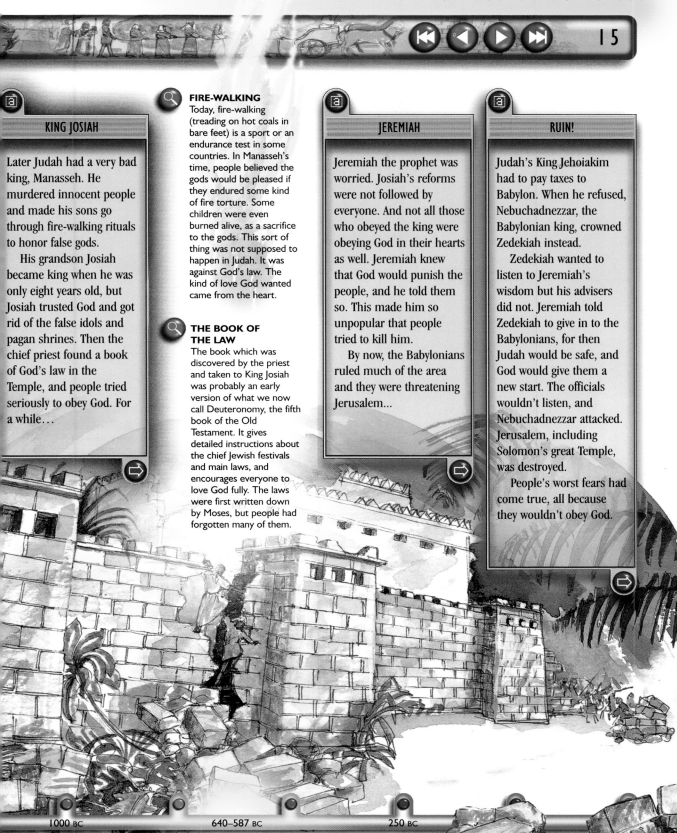

KING JOSIAH

Later Judah had a very bad king, Manasseh. He murdered innocent people and made his sons go through fire-walking rituals to honor false gods.

His grandson Josiah became king when he was only eight years old, but Josiah trusted God and got rid of the false idols and pagan shrines. Then the chief priest found a book of God's law in the Temple, and people tried seriously to obey God. For a while…

FIRE-WALKING

Today, fire-walking (treading on hot coals in bare feet) is a sport or an endurance test in some countries. In Manasseh's time, people believed the gods would be pleased if they endured some kind of fire torture. Some children were even burned alive, as a sacrifice to the gods. This sort of thing was not supposed to happen in Judah. It was against God's law. The kind of love God wanted came from the heart.

THE BOOK OF THE LAW

The book which was discovered by the priest and taken to King Josiah was probably an early version of what we now call Deuteronomy, the fifth book of the Old Testament. It gives detailed instructions about the chief Jewish festivals and main laws, and encourages everyone to love God fully. The laws were first written down by Moses, but people had forgotten many of them.

JEREMIAH

Jeremiah the prophet was worried. Josiah's reforms were not followed by everyone. And not all those who obeyed the king were obeying God in their hearts as well. Jeremiah knew that God would punish the people, and he told them so. This made him so unpopular that people tried to kill him.

By now, the Babylonians ruled much of the area and they were threatening Jerusalem…

RUIN!

Judah's King Jehoiakim had to pay taxes to Babylon. When he refused, Nebuchadnezzar, the Babylonian king, crowned Zedekiah instead.

Zedekiah wanted to listen to Jeremiah's wisdom but his advisers did not. Jeremiah told Zedekiah to give in to the Babylonians, for then Judah would be safe, and God would give them a new start. The officials wouldn't listen, and Nebuchadnezzar attacked. Jerusalem, including Solomon's great Temple, was destroyed.

People's worst fears had come true, all because they wouldn't obey God.

1000 BC   640–587 BC   250 BC

A LONG WAY FROM HOME

For almost twenty years, King Nebuchadnezzar of Babylon had attacked Judah and gradually taken most of the leaders and thousands of people away to Babylon as prisoners of war. By 587 BC when his army completely destroyed Jerusalem, Ezekiel, a priest, had been in Babylon for some time. The last group of exiles arrived, having made a journey of nearly 600 miles. They were deeply sad...

BABYLON

Babylon was a large and beautiful city. King Nebuchadnezzar had built a huge palace for his wife. It had gardens and waterfalls on the rooftops, know as the "hanging gardens". The Ishtar Gate in the city wall was decorated with dragons, bulls and other animals. There were huge temples dedicated to many different gods.

A VISION OF GOD

God sent them some messages to cheer them up. When Ezekiel was in Babylon, God called him to be a prophet. He had a great vision of God: a vision of wheels moving in all directions. The wheels had eyes all over them.

It meant that God had traveled all the way to Babylon with them! God could see what was happening. God hadn't left them after all.

BABYLONIAN GODS

The Babylonians had many gods, which caused a problem for the Jews. The chief god was Anu, the god of heaven. Ishtar was the goddess of love. The moon god was called Sin and the sun god Shamash. The Jews worked hard to keep their belief in the one true God.

IN BABYLON

The exiles from Judah were herded into camps by the rivers and canals.

The Babylonians asked them to sing their folk songs, but all they wanted to do was cry. It seemed as if God had left them. They hung their harps on trees; their music was silenced as if they were mourning.

They felt like giving up.

VISIONS

God spoke to Ezekiel through many visions. They were like dreams, in which the prophet saw pictures. It was God's way of helping him to understand what was happening and what God planned to do. Several other prophets had visions, too, including Jeremiah and Daniel.

HOPE FOR THE FUTURE

There was hope for the future too. Another of Ezekiel's visions was of a valley full of skeletons. God told him to prophesy to the bones. In the vision, God covered the bones with flesh, then made them come alive.

Ezekiel realised that God's Spirit would make his chosen people "come alive" in a new way. But where and when would that be?

SETTLE DOWN

Some prophets said that God would rescue God's people from Babylon soon. Jeremiah disagreed. He had stayed in Jerusalem.

Not long after the exiles had left for Babylon, Jeremiah wrote them a letter. He told them not to listen to the prophets – instead, they should stay in Babylon, settle down and build new lives. God would allow them home – but they had to trust God.

SCRIBES AND THE SYNAGOGUE

During this period of "the exile", as it is known, the Jewish religion that we see in the New Testament began to take the shape. The scribes began to copy out and teach the scriptures. As there was no Temple, the people began meeting in small groups (synagogues) to pray and hear the scriptures.

DANIEL AND FRIENDS

One of the exiles was Daniel. He and his three friends were very clever, so the king gave them important jobs in the government. Daniel was able to interpret dreams and became a powerful leader.

But when jealous Babylonians tried to trap them, the four Jews stayed true to God even if it meant dying. Daniel escaped from a den of lions, and the three friends survived a blazing furnace.

Daniel in the lions' den.

TORTURE AND DEATH

Babylonian kings kept lions in little zoos. For fun, they would chase them in a paddock. When they wanted to punish people, they just fed them to the lions. Another punishment was throwing people into a pottery kiln, which was very, very hot. When Daniel and his friends survived these punishments, it was a sign that the people of God would be kept safe.

HOME AT LAST

The Jews in Babylon did what Jeremiah had told them. They settled down, had families and worked hard. Eventually, Jeremiah's words came true. There was a change of government in Babylon, and the Persians took over the country. The first thing that King Cyrus did on taking power in 538 BC was to allow all exiles, including the Jews, to go back to their own countries if they wanted to…

 THE JOURNEY BACK
There were no proper roads across the Babylonian Empire, only tracks used by armies and merchants. The direct way to Jerusalem ran from east to west, but it was across a desert. The exiles had to go north and follow what is called the fertile crescent. It was about 900 miles (1450 km) – a long walk.

BACK TO JERUSALEM

Many of the people in exile returned to Jerusalem and started to rebuild the Temple. They laid the foundations and started offering sacrifices again.

The whole place was a ruin. They had to build their own houses, find work and start growing food, too. Even worse, the local people hated them and tried to stop the work on the Temple.

At that point they got fed up, and the building work stopped.

 **THE WALLS OF JERUSALEM**
These were important for two reasons. The walls helped protect the city against attackers, and soldiers could stand on them and repel invaders. The walls also helped the people feel that Jerusalem was a proper city.

 THE SECOND TEMPLE
The first Temple built by Solomon had been large and splendid. This second Temple built by Zerubbabel was smaller but built on the same pattern: an inner room (the Most Holy Place) where the high priest alone was allowed to enter, and an outer room (the Holy Place). In the courtyard outside was the altar of burned offering.

2250 BC   2000 BC   1750 BC   1500 BC   1250 BC

Esther was married to Xerxes, king of Persia.

IN RUINS

Then the prophets Haggai and Zechariah began preaching, saying it was a scandal that people had nice houses but that God's Temple was still in ruins. The local people tried to oppose them, but the Jews started work on the Temple once again.

THANKSGIVING

Within four years the Temple was finished. It was dedicated to God in a great ceremony. They sacrificed hundreds of animals as an act of thanksgiving to God. And for the first time since they returned to Judah, the people celebrated the annual Passover festival.

ESTHER

Meanwhile in Susa, a city of the Persian Empire, trouble was brewing. An evil man called Haman tried to make the Persian king pass a rule that would let him kill all the Jews in the whole world. Esther, his queen, was a Jew and, when she found out about the plot from her cousin Mordecai, she revealed Haman's plan to the king. The king made sure the Jews were saved.

NEHEMIAH

One of the exiles in Susa was Nehemiah, the king's wine-taster. When he heard that Jerusalem still didn't have proper city walls, he was horrified. He got permission to go straight back to Jerusalem, where he got everyone working together to build up the walls and make the city secure. When Nehemiah prayed, God gave him success.

THE PERSIANS

The Persians took over the Babylonian Empire, allowing the Jews to return to Judah. Many Jews stayed on and some, like Nehemiah and Ezra, became high officials. The Persians divided the empire into regions with governors called "satraps". The Greeks under Alexander the Great took over the empire in 331 BC.

Zechariah's vision.

ZECHARIAH

Zechariah's prophecies used lots of pictures to help people understand God's messages. In a vision about a man on a red horse, God promised to restore God's people, their towns and the Temple.

1000 BC   750 BC   538–440 BC

A KING IS BORN IN A STABLE

For many years people in Judea had been expecting God to send the *Messiah*, his special agent, to bring God's peace to the world and to start a new society. They thought of him as a military king, like David. But God had other ideas, so when the Messiah was born, hardly anyone noticed...

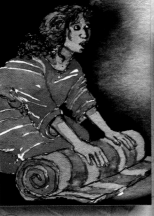

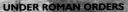
Mary was just a young girl when the angel came to her.

MARY

The first person to hear the news couldn't believe her ears.

Mary was engaged to be married. One day she saw an angel who said God had chosen her to be the mother of the Messiah. God would make the baby grow inside her.

Then there was a problem...

BETHLEHEM

The Romans ordered a census. Everyone had to go to their ancestors' home town to be registered for taxes.

Mary was heavily pregnant; she and her husband Joseph had to travel a long way to Bethlehem but there was nowhere to stay.

Mary gave birth to Jesus in the place where the animals were kept. Meanwhile...

MESSENGERS FROM GOD
Angels are God's messengers. They appeared at special times to tell people what God was doing, or to help people in difficult situations. Sometimes they appeared looking like the people of the time; at other times, like this, they seemed to be dazzling white.

THE FAMILY OF DAVID
Mary was a simple country girl, living in a village in the hills called Nazareth. She was engaged to Joseph, the village carpenter. Both Mary and Joseph were descendants of King David. The Jews believed that the Messiah would come from the family line of David.

UNDER ROMAN ORDERS
The Romans ordered all the people in their lands to return to the place their family came from to be counted. Mary and Joseph had to travel to Bethlehem where their ancestors had come from. Bethlehem was a small village not far from Jerusalem.

The Romans ordered the people to return to their ancestors' home towns for a census.

PRE-HISTORY   2000 BC   1750 BC   1500 BC   1250 BC

ESCAPE

Herod was afraid of a rival, so he had all little boys aged under two years old killed.

But Joseph had been warned about this in a dream, and he took Mary and Jesus to Egypt.

After Herod's death they returned safely to Nazareth where Jesus grew up.

SHEPHERDS

Out in the fields, an angel appeared to some shepherds. They were amazed.

The angel said that the Messiah had been born in the village. So they left their flocks of sheep and went to see the baby.

Much later, some other strange visitors came...

WISE MEN

They were Magi, priests or wise men from the east.

They believed Jesus' birth had been announced by a special star, and they came to honor the "king of the Jews". They brought expensive presents.

But they went first to Jerusalem, expecting to find the baby there. They told King Herod, who wasn't pleased...

THE SHEPHERDS
Shepherds protected their sheep from wild animals, so usually they never left their sheep alone. But after the angel's visit, they just had to go and see the baby King.

THE STAR
No one knows exactly what the special star was. Some people think it was a super nova or exploding star, and others a conjunction of Saturn and Jupiter, which might have looked like one bright star. Others think it might have been a comet, or a pattern of stars.

Herod the Great.

MURDEROUS HEROD
King Herod was governor of Galilee. The Romans gave him the title of king of the Jews, and he ruled from 37 to 4 BC. He was not Jewish by birth, and was afraid of anyone whom he saw as a threat to his position. He was guilty not only of the deaths of the babies at the time of Jesus' birth, but also of killing most of his own family.

500 BC   250 BC   4 BC–0 AD

"TURN BACK TO GOD!"

Jesus' mother Mary had a relative called Elizabeth who was married to Zechariah, a priest. One day, when Zechariah was in the Temple, he saw an angel who told him they would have a son called John who would prepare the way for the Messiah. Zechariah couldn't believe it, and was unable to speak until the baby was born. When he grew up, John had a job to do…

JOHN THE BAPTIST
John wore animal skins and lived in the desert. He ate whatever he could find, including locusts and wild honey.

GET READY

John lived rough in the desert.

People came from miles around to hear his fiery preaching. He told people to turn back to God because the Messiah was coming.

He baptized the people in the River Jordan.

John baptized Jesus.

THE RIVER JORDAN

The River Jordan flows from Lake Galilee in the north to the Dead Sea in the south. The part where John baptized people is quite shallow and people can wade across it. It was some distance from Jerusalem, so it was a sign of people's interest that they were willing to travel to hear John speak.

BAPTISM

Baptism is a ceremony that Christians still use as a sign of faith and membership of the church today. It is a symbol of God's "cleansing" or forgiveness of someone's sins, and their willingness to live God's way. People are fully immersed in water, or sprinkled with it. In some churches, babies are baptized as well as adults; in others, only adults are baptized.

THE DEVIL

Christians believe that the devil, or Satan, is a spiritual being who was once one of God's angels. For some reason, probably out of pride, he rebelled against God and was thrown out of heaven. Ever since, he has tried to stop God's work. He is not as powerful as God. One of the reasons Jesus died on the cross and rose from death was to break the hold of Satan over people's lives.

THE DEATH OF JOHN

Then John the Baptist was put in prison. He had criticised King Herod Antipas for having married in a way that broke God's law.

Then Herod's step-daughter Salome pleased Herod so much by her dancing that he offered her anything she wanted.

She asked for John the Baptist to be killed...

TWELVE MEN

Jesus started calling people to be his disciples. In Galilee he chose twelve men to be his special helpers. Among them were Peter and Andrew, two brothers, and their fishing partners, James and John.

Jesus told these fishermen, "From now on, you'll catch people for God."

Another of his disciples was Matthew, a tax collector for the Romans, a job most people despised.

THE MESSIAH

One day, Jesus came to be baptized. John recognised him at once, not just as his cousin, but as the Messiah.

"You're the Lamb of God who's come to take away the sin of the world," John exclaimed. "You ought to baptize me!"

But Jesus insisted. When he came out of the water, a dove settled on him, as a sign of God's Spirit, and a voice from heaven said, "This is my own dear Son."

IN THE DESERT

Then Jesus went into the desert. He spent six weeks there praying to God his Father, eating nothing and preparing for his work.

At the end of that time he was tempted by the devil to use his powers for his own needs: to make bread, to impress people and to get power for himself. They were strong temptations, but Jesus said no, and then he went into Galilee to start telling people about God's kingdom.

Jesus spent a lot of time praying to his Father.

TEMPTATION

Temptation describes the feeling of wanting to do something which a person knows is wrong, or forbidden by God. Disobeying God is called sin. The Bible says that God always provides people who are tempted with the strength to say no, if they ask. God also offers forgiveness for all who ask for it.

LIVING GOD'S WAY

Wherever Jesus went, crowds followed him. They had never heard anyone teach the way he did. He told simple stories which had deep and important meanings. The official teachers gave people lots of rules to follow. Jesus told people that God was like a loving Father, not a stern slave driver. Here are some of his teachings...

Jesus welcomed the children.

PHARISEES

They were a small group of religious leaders who believed that God would only be pleased if people kept every one of God's rules completely. To help people keep them, Pharisees had made over 600 more rules about how to keep the main ones! Jesus challenged their views; God wanted people to be obedient, but God also wanted them to be loving. When they failed, God was always ready to forgive them.

A LOVING PARENT

Jesus said that God loves people, whatever they have done.

Jesus told a story about a young man who wasted all his father's money, then came home begging for forgiveness. The father threw a party!

"My son's alive!" he said. "That's all that matters."

God welcomes people who ask for forgiveness, Jesus said.

BE KIND

God is kind and expects us to be kind too.

Jesus told a story about a Jew who was robbed. Some people who thought they were very holy and religious left him to die on the roadside. They didn't want to get involved. But a Samaritan (an enemy of the Jews) stopped to help him.

"Everyone's your neighbour," Jesus said, "so help anyone in need."

SAMARITANS

Samaria was an area of central Judea, between Jerusalem and Galilee. The Jews hated the Samaritans because they were of mixed race and they didn't believe all the things Jews believed. Jesus visited Samaria, but most Jews avoided it. They would travel round it rather than through it, even though it took them much longer.

GOD'S KINGDOM

God is King of a special kingdom, Jesus said. God's kingdom isn't a small place but covers the whole world. It exists wherever there are people who love and serve God.

Jesus said God is sowing truth in people's lives like a farmer sows seed in the ground. Sometimes it takes root and sometimes it doesn't. But when it does it produces a "harvest" of love and kindness.

DON'T WORRY

Jesus said God was like a loving parent who gave good things to his children and never wanted to hurt them. He told people to depend on God.

"Don't worry about everyday things," Jesus said. "You'll never go without them just because you give your time to serving God."

GRAINFIELDS

Wheat and barley grew in the fields in Galilee to provide people with bread, a staple part of their diet. Jesus often used grainfields as a picture of God's kingdom: just as weeds grow alongside the grain, so good and bad people live side by side in the world.

Jesus taught his friends about God over a period of about three years.

THE SERMON ON THE MOUNT

Jesus often taught out on the hillsides by Lake Galilee, and Matthew's Gospel records "the sermon on the mount". Jesus told his friends how to live God's way. He looked around at the wild flowers and the birds and told people not to worry about their future, because God would look after them, just as God looked after the plants and animals.

I WILL RETURN

Jesus often spoke about his coming death.

But he said that after he had died and had risen from death, he would return to earth at some unknown time in the future to judge the world. It will be like when a shepherd separates sheep and goats at a water hole, he said. God will separate those who have loved God from those who haven't.

JESUS' RETURN

Jesus often said he would come back to earth one day. But he also said that no one could ever know when it would be. It would be sudden and unexpected, but everyone would know – it wouldn't be a secret coming like his birth in Bethlehem.

1000 BC   750 BC   250 BC   AD 30–33

"IT'S A MIRACLE!"

Jesus didn't simply tell people that God cared for them, he showed it too. He was always ready to talk to people, especially people who did not fit in to society, because he wanted to show God loved all people. He healed people and did other miracles too. Each act was a message in itself...

EVIL SPIRITS
The Bible teaches that Jesus came to defeat evil. Jesus showed he had the power to defeat all kinds of evil.

A MAD MAN

Some of Jesus' healings were spectacular.

Out in the country was a wild man who lived in caves. He was so strong no one could keep him chained. Jesus knew that the man was tormented by evil spirits. He told the spirits to leave the man and go into a herd of pigs, which they did. The man was calm after that.

This showed that Jesus came to destroy evil and give people a new start.

A teacher at the synagogue.

SYNAGOGUES
The synagogue is where Jewish people meet each Sabbath (Saturday) to pray, and hear the scriptures read and taught. Jesus sometimes taught in synagogues. Archaeologists have found the remains of a first-century synagogue in Capernaum, the town in Galilee where Jesus lived as an adult.

A BLIND MAN

A man who had been born blind met Jesus on the roadside. People believed that all illness was because of someone's sin.

"So whose sin caused this?" they asked. "The man's sin, or his parents' sin?"

"Neither," Jesus said, and healed him.

He showed that God hated the suffering that came from evil in the world, and wanted to put it right.

1750 BC   1500 BC   1250 BC

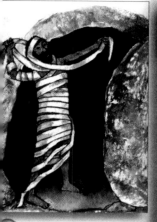

Lazarus had been in the tomb for four days when Jesus arrived in Bethany.

LAZARUS

Lazarus and his sisters, Mary and Martha, were special friends to Jesus. When Lazarus became ill, Jesus didn't go to see him until he had died. Martha was angry.

"You could have healed him!" she said to Jesus.

Jesus wept at the sadness and evil of death, but then he brought Lazarus back to life.

He told Martha, "I am the resurrection and the life. Whoever trusts in me will live for ever."

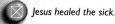

Jesus healed the sick.

FISHING

On Lake Galilee two methods of fishing were used. The fishermen either waded into the water and threw out their nets by hand, or they went out in boats, dragging nets along in the water.

LOAVES AND FISHES

The loaves which belonged to the boy at the picnic were small (like large rolls) and made from barley (which poorer people used). The fish would probably have been dried, and were also quite small. The Bible says that Jesus' disciples picked up twelve baskets of leftovers afterwards.

THE BIG PICNIC

One day Jesus fed a crowd of more than 5,000 people. Having taught people out in the hills all day, he asked his disciples to give them something to eat.

"You're joking!" they cried. "We couldn't afford it!"

Andrew found a boy with five loaves and two fish. It seemed so little for so many people. But when Jesus took them and shared them out, everyone had enough to eat.

THE GREAT STORM

Jesus was once in a boat on Lake Galilee with his friends when a great storm blew up. Jesus was sleeping soundly.

When his terrified friends woke him up, afraid they would drown, he simply stood up and told the storm to stop. It did. Only God could command the weather, so it showed his friends that Jesus must be God as well as human.

LAKE GALILEE

This is a large inland lake surrounded by hills also called the Sea of Gallilee. Sometimes there are sudden and violent storms. The lake is rich in fish and in Jesus' day fishermen caught so many that they were able to export salted and dried fish.

JESUS IS CRUCIFIED

People either loved Jesus or they hated him. They could not ignore him. He was a popular teacher and healer and people came from miles around to hear him. But some religious and political leaders were jealous of his popularity. They thought his teaching was wrong. And they were afraid he might stir up trouble with the Romans.

So they plotted to kill him...

JESUS THE KING

A week before the Passover festival, Jesus entered Jerusalem riding a donkey. People threw down their cloaks and waved palm branches like flags.

"Blessed is he who comes in God's name!" they cheered.

They welcomed him like a king. It made the religious leaders – the Pharisees – angry, but there was nothing they could do.

Jesus entered Jerusalem on a donkey.

JESUS IN THE TEMPLE

Then Jesus went to the Temple where officials were selling doves for the religious sacrifices, and changing money in the Court of the Gentiles. Jesus tipped over the tables and drove out the traders.

"My Father's house shall be a house of prayer," he cried. "but you've made it a den of thieves."

At this, the religious leaders were even more angry.

The Passover feast.

THE PASSOVER
This annual Jewish festival celebrates the exodus of the Israelites from Egypt led by Moses. During the meal, symbolic actions reminded people of important truths. Jesus gave two of them – the shared bread and wine – a new meaning, which is continued in the Christian service of Holy Communion.

GETHSEMANE
This was an olive grove, which may have been owned by the family of John Mark, who later became a helper with Paul and who wrote Mark's Gospel. The Gospel says there was a young man in the olive grove when the soldiers arrived. He fled naked. This may have been Mark, who would have been sleeping in the watchman's hut.

Judas betrayed Jesus with a kiss.

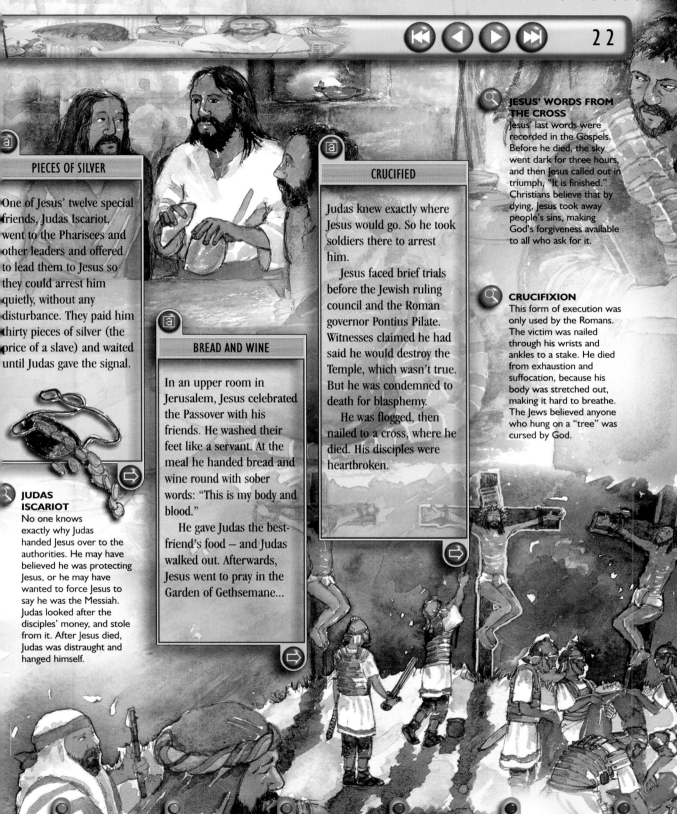

PIECES OF SILVER

One of Jesus' twelve special friends, Judas Iscariot, went to the Pharisees and other leaders and offered to lead them to Jesus so they could arrest him quietly, without any disturbance. They paid him thirty pieces of silver (the price of a slave) and waited until Judas gave the signal.

JUDAS ISCARIOT
No one knows exactly why Judas handed Jesus over to the authorities. He may have believed he was protecting Jesus, or he may have wanted to force Jesus to say he was the Messiah. Judas looked after the disciples' money, and stole from it. After Jesus died, Judas was distraught and hanged himself.

BREAD AND WINE

In an upper room in Jerusalem, Jesus celebrated the Passover with his friends. He washed their feet like a servant. At the meal he handed bread and wine round with sober words: "This is my body and blood."

He gave Judas the best-friend's food – and Judas walked out. Afterwards, Jesus went to pray in the Garden of Gethsemane...

CRUCIFIED

Judas knew exactly where Jesus would go. So he took soldiers there to arrest him.

Jesus faced brief trials before the Jewish ruling council and the Roman governor Pontius Pilate. Witnesses claimed he had said he would destroy the Temple, which wasn't true. But he was condemned to death for blasphemy.

He was flogged, then nailed to a cross, where he died. His disciples were heartbroken.

JESUS' WORDS FROM THE CROSS
Jesus' last words were recorded in the Gospels. Before he died, the sky went dark for three hours, and then Jesus called out in triumph, "It is finished." Christians believe that by dying, Jesus took away people's sins, making God's forgiveness available to all who ask for it.

CRUCIFIXION
This form of execution was only used by the Romans. The victim was nailed through his wrists and ankles to a stake. He died from exhaustion and suffocation, because his body was stretched out, making it hard to breathe. The Jews believed anyone who hung on a "tree" was cursed by God.

1000 BC   750 BC   500 BC   250 BC   AD 33

JESUS IS RISEN!

Jesus' disciples were heartbroken. Their leader was dead. All their hopes were shattered. How could God let such a thing happen? They were frightened too; they thought they would be killed next. So they went into hiding. But two days later, something happened which took them all by surprise...

MARY

When Mary saw the empty tomb, she was upset. Had Jesus' body been taken from the tomb? Alone, she stood crying near the tomb. Someone came up to her. She thought he was the gardener.

"What's wrong?" he asked.

She replied, "Tell me where the body is."

The figure said, "Mary."

She jumped. She knew the voice. It was Jesus! Delighted, but also confused, she ran to tell the others...

THE EMPTY TOMB

Early on the Sunday morning, Mary Magdalene and some other women went to the tomb. It belonged to Joseph of Arimathea, a rich Jew who had followed Jesus.

The women wanted to wrap Jesus' body up properly, because there hadn't been time before the Sabbath. But when they got there, the stone across the tomb had been moved.

They called Peter and John, who investigated. The body was gone...

TOMB
Inside the rock tomb, there was a shelf where the body was laid. A heavy stone was rolled in a groove, like a sliding door, across the entrance to the tomb.

BURIAL
In the hot climate, people were buried the same day they died, before the body began to decay. The body was wrapped in bandages with layers of spices in between, like a mummy. The body was usually put in a tomb cut from the rock, or in a cave. It was not buried in the ground because it was too stony, and wild animals might dig up the body.

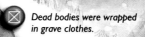
Dead bodies were wrapped in grave clothes.

Cleopas and his companion recognised Jesus as he broke the bread.

JESUS BY THE LAKE

One morning, after the disciples had been out fishing all night, they saw a man at the lakeside, with bread and fish cooking on a fire. Peter knew at once it was Jesus, and jumped out of the boat. It was the third time they had seen Jesus after his resurrection.

RESURRECTION

No one else has ever come back from the dead like Jesus. Inside the tomb, the cloths in which the body had been wrapped were left, looking as though the body had risen through them. The head-covering was also complete and left folded. The risen Jesus appeared to his disciples with a body; he was not a ghost. He even ate meals with his friends.

DOUBTING THOMAS

Jesus appeared to his disciples in the upper room in Jerusalem on the day he rose from the dead. One of them, Thomas, wasn't there. He found it hard to believe and said he'd never believe it unless he saw Jesus for himself. A few days later Jesus came again to the upper room. When Thomas saw Jesus, he worshipped him as God.

WERE THEY MISTAKEN?

It is not possible to prove in a scientific way that Jesus rose from death. But there is lots of evidence. The body was never found, and the grave clothes were not disturbed.

JESUS IS ALIVE

The other disciples didn't believe it!

Then Jesus came and stood in the middle of the locked room where most of them were gathered together.

They were terrified at first because they thought he was a ghost. But they couldn't deny he was alive, although they didn't understand it.

THE ROAD TO EMMAUS

The same day, in the evening, two people were leaving Jerusalem along the Emmaus Road. They were joined by another traveller, and they told him their sadness about Jesus' death.

"Didn't you realise the scriptures said this would happen?" the stranger asked.

At Emmaus, they sat down to eat together, and when the man thanked God for the food, they realised it was Jesus!

Then he disappeared, so they rushed back to Jerusalem...

THE ASCENSION

For six more weeks Jesus kept appearing to people. He told the disciples all they needed to know about what to do when he was gone.

Then one day they went up on a hillside, and Jesus said goodbye because he was going back to be with God.

He disappeared from view, telling them to wait until the Holy Spirit came to help them.

1000 BC   750 BC   500 BC   250 BC   AD 33

THE CHURCH IS BORN

After the risen Jesus left them, the disciples didn't know what to expect. But they waited in Jerusalem for the Holy Spirit, the "helper" he had promised. So while they waited, they met together regularly to pray. They elected Matthias to take the place of Judas among the twelve, now known as apostles. And then came the Jewish festival of Pentecost...

PENTECOST

This Jewish festival to celebrate the barley harvest, held fifty days after the Passover, was also called the "Feast of Weeks". People traveled from all over the known world to Jerusalem to celebrate it, so the message of Jesus was heard by thousands.

3,000 BELIEVERS

As the disciples made such a noise praying, a crowd of people gathered. Some thought they had been drinking too much. Peter told the crowd how Jesus had been crucified, then raised from the dead, and now he had sent his promised Spirit. They should give their lives to Jesus, he said. Amazingly, about 3,000 did, and that was just the start…

THE SPIRIT COMES

That morning a group of the disciples were praying together when suddenly, they felt something in the room. There was a strong gale of wind. It looked as if people glowed and there were flames on people's heads. They all began to speak God's words in other languages.

The Holy Spirit had come!

Peter speaks out for the first time after Pentecost.

HEALING MIRACLES

The apostles healed people, just as Jesus had done. People laid the sick on mats in the streets, hoping that Peter's shadow might fall on them. At the gate called Beautiful, Peter healed a lame man.

STEPHEN

Stephen was a good preacher, and God used him to do a number of miracles. He was arrested by the authorities and put on trial.

Then he was stoned to death for blasphemy: the first Christian martyr to die for his faith.

Watching it all was a young, zealous Jew called Saul, who hated Christians…

PETER AND JOHN

Some of the religious leaders in Jerusalem were worried when they saw how many people were becoming followers of Jesus.

When the apostles healed people, just as Jesus had done, the leaders tried to stop them. They arrested Peter and John, but the apostles were eventually released, and went straight back to preaching.

A NEW WAY

The first Christians met together regularly to pray, to sing, and to hear the apostles explain the scriptures and how they should live. They shared their belongings with each other and cared for those who were poor. They appointed seven people to look after the practical things so the apostles could preach and teach, but life was hard…

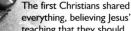

SHARING TOGETHER

The first Christians shared everything, believing Jesus' teaching that they should help others. This sharing was called "fellowship". People prayed for each other, encouraged each other and helped each other. A group of Christians was called a church.

STONING

This was the traditional Jewish way of executing someone for religious and other crimes. In fact, the killing of Stephen was probably illegal. Only the Romans were supposed to execute people, which is why Jesus had been crucified by them, even though the charges were really religious. The victim was probably half buried in a hole, and the chief accuser threw the first stone.

 Saul watched the stoning of Stephen.

 1000 BC   750 BC   250 BC   AD 30–35

PAUL THE PREACHER

Saul of Tarsus watched Stephen being killed with great satisfaction. He hated the Christians. And the Christians were afraid of him. He was a faithful Jew who knew the scriptures backwards. He thought Christians were making false claims about Jesus, so he got permission to hunt them down and, if possible, to get them executed. One day, he was on the road to Damascus, when something happened...

SAUL OF TARSUS

Saul was born a Roman citizen, with Jewish parents. He had studied under the Pharisee, Gamaliel, for many years and was regarded as bright and a future leader. Like all educated Jews, he had a manual skill as well – he was a tent-maker. He used his skill to earn his food while he was travelling.

"SAUL! SAUL!"

Saul was stopped in his tracks by a bright light. He heard a voice saying to him, "Saul! Saul! Why are you persecuting me?"

It was the risen Jesus, appearing especially to him.

The light blinded Saul, so his friends took him into Damascus. There a Christian named Ananias prayed for him, and he could see again.

PAUL

Saul's former friends wanted to kill him for becoming a traitor so the Christians smuggled him out of the city in a basket. His name was changed to Paul, and some years later God called him to travel to new places telling people about Jesus.

He was known now as an apostle. He made three great journeys, with different companions.

They were all action-packed…

The Temple of Artemis.

Places Paul visited.

PHILIPPI

This was a large city in northern Greece. It was regarded by the Romans as being part of Italy (even though it wasn't), so all its people had the rights of Roman citizens. Many military officers went to live there when they retired. It was famous for its gold products.

The Philippian jailer.

1750 BC   1500 BC

MISTAKEN FOR GODS

At Iconium, their opponents tried to kill them – a threat Paul survived many times over the years.

In Lystra, Paul and Barnabas healed a lame man in the name of Jesus. As a result, people thought they were the Roman gods Zeus and Hermes!

The local priest even tried to offer the apostles an animal sacrifice.

IN PRISON AGAIN

In Philippi (on his second journey), Paul and his friend Silas healed a girl who had an evil spirit. Because she had earned a lot of money by her strange powers, her owners stirred up a riot when she lost her powers.

The apostles were jailed, but an earthquake broke their chains. The apostles didn't run away, the jailer and his family became believers and the magistrates apologised and let them go.

VISITING

On his third journey, Paul visited many places and spent nearly three years in Ephesus. That visit ended in a huge riot in the city's arena, but he went on to visit some of the other churches.

In one visit, at Troas, a young man named Eutychus fell asleep as Paul was teaching, and fell out of a high window. He was dead, but Paul restored him and he lived, much to everyone's relief!

ROMAN GODS
Zeus was thought of as the chief god, and Hermes was his spokesman. The people of Lystra had a legend that the two gods had come there once but no one recognised them except an old couple. Consequently they were always looking out for them again! When they saw Paul and Barnabas healing the lame man, they thought the gods had come back.

EPHESUS
Ephesus was a splendid city, now in modern-day Turkey. It had a long wide road leading from its harbor to the city center. The temple to Artemis or Diana in Ephesus was one of the seven wonders of the world, and the theatre or arena where Paul was taken held 25,000 people.

BARNABAS
Barnabas introduced Paul to the other apostles, and then worked with Paul with the non-Jewish people of Antioch. Later, he supported his nephew Mark who had gone home in the middle of Paul's first journey, much to Paul's anger.

PAUL'S LETTERS
Paul cared for the churches he started. He sent his helpers to look after them, and wrote letters to them too. In one letter he wrote to the churches in the Roman province of Galatia. False teachers told them that Christians had to follow Jewish customs. Nonsense, said Paul. All you need is faith in Jesus.

1000 BC   750 BC   500 BC   250 BC   AD 35–57

PAUL TRAVELS TO ROME

Paul had wanted to visit Rome for a long time. There were already a lot of Christians there. He wanted to teach them more about following Jesus, and then go from Rome on a journey further west to Spain. No one knows if he got to Spain or not, but he did get to Rome. And it was not in the way he expected…

ROMAN ARMY
Paul was guarded and protected by Roman soldiers. They were like a police force as well as fighters who put down rebellions. The Roman army was well organised into groups of 100 men (a century). A cohort was formed of between five and eight centuries, and a legion numbered about 5,500 men.

SHIPS
Most ships in Roman times carried cargo and passengers. They were not big by modern standards, but remarkably big for the time: maybe up to around 60 yards lon. The ship Paul was in carried 276 passenger. Because of the dangers, few ships sailed on the Mediterranean between October and April. They were powered by sails and oars

ROME
A large city built on seven hills near the mouth of the River Tiber, Rome had been important for 700 years before Paul's time. It was the seat of government for the whole empire, and was full of big temples, arenas and housing.

Paul preached to huge crowds.

ROMAN CITIZEN

After his third journey Paul went to Jerusalem, even though a prophet warned that he would be arrested i he did.

Not long after he arrived, he was recognised and falsely accused of breaking Jewish law. A riot broke out and he was arrested by the Romans. He told them he was a Roman citizen, and they treated him well. In fact, they saved his life…

1750 BC   1500 BC   1250 BC

SHIPWRECK!

The journey was a disaster. The ship sailed late in the year, was caught in a storm and was wrecked off the coast of the island of Malta. No one perished though, and the people of Malta looked after them all.

On the island, Paul prayed for the governor's father, who got well after a serious illness.

After three months, they sailed for Rome in another ship.

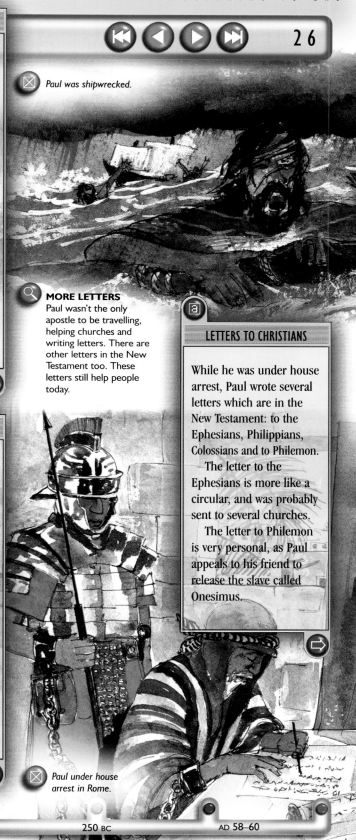

Paul was shipwrecked.

TO ROME

Some of the people in Jerusalem who hated Christians made a secret plan to kill Paul, but his nephew heard about it. He told the Romans who had arrested Paul, and they took him under armed guard to Caesarea.

There, Paul was tried before two Roman governors and the Jewish king Herod Agrippa, who thought he was mad but harmless! Because Paul had appealed for a trial before the emperor they sent him off to Rome.

ROMAN CHRISTIANS
Christians were forced to leave the city, along with many Jews, in the middle of the first century. When they returned the Emperor Nero killed many of them, including Paul and Peter, between AD 64 and 68.

HOUSE ARREST

Christians from Rome came to the coast to meet Paul and his friends, and went with them on the last bit of the journey. In Rome Paul was held under house arrest. He could have visitors, and many came to hear about Jesus. It is possible, but not certain, that he was released for a while, went to some of the western churches and perhaps to Spain, before being executed in about AD 67.

Paul under house arrest in Rome.

MORE LETTERS
Paul wasn't the only apostle to be travelling, helping churches and writing letters. There are other letters in the New Testament too. These letters still help people today.

LETTERS TO CHRISTIANS

While he was under house arrest, Paul wrote several letters which are in the New Testament: to the Ephesians, Philippians, Colossians and to Philemon.

The letter to the Ephesians is more like a circular, and was probably sent to several churches.

The letter to Philemon is very personal, as Paul appeals to his friend to release the slave called Onesimus.

LOOKING FORWARD TO THE END

Christians in the first century had a hard time. People did not like their claim that Jesus was the only way to God, and so they were persecuted – arrested, put in prison, and even killed. John's Book of Revelation encouraged the Christians to keep going, even though everything around them seemed to be falling apart…

A VISION OF JESUS

Revelation is not like other Bible books: it is full of strange picture language, and not easy for anyone to understand. At first John sees a great vision of Jesus. Later the whole book is a series of visions, a bit like a window into heaven and eternity. As John looks through it, he sees something of what God is doing through human history and the whole of time.

JOHN THE PRISONER

The apostle John was an old man when he had this series of visions. He had been a church leader in Ephesus, but was arrested and put in a prison camp on the isle of Patmos, in the Aegean Sea.

THE SEVEN CHURCHES

First, there are special messages from Jesus to seven churches in Asia Minor, the area in which John had lived and worked. Each message picks out some weakness or strength in the church and encourages the Christians to stay faithful to Jesus. If they don't, he warns, the churches will cease to exist.

FOUR HORSES

Revelation uses numbers as signs. Four and seven are both signs that mean "complete" or "all". So the four horses stand for "all the world's suffering". One horse stands for abuse of political power, one for war, one for famine, and one for death.

Map labels: Pergamum, Thyatira, Smyrna, Sardis, Philadelphia, Ephesus, Laodicea, Patmos (island)

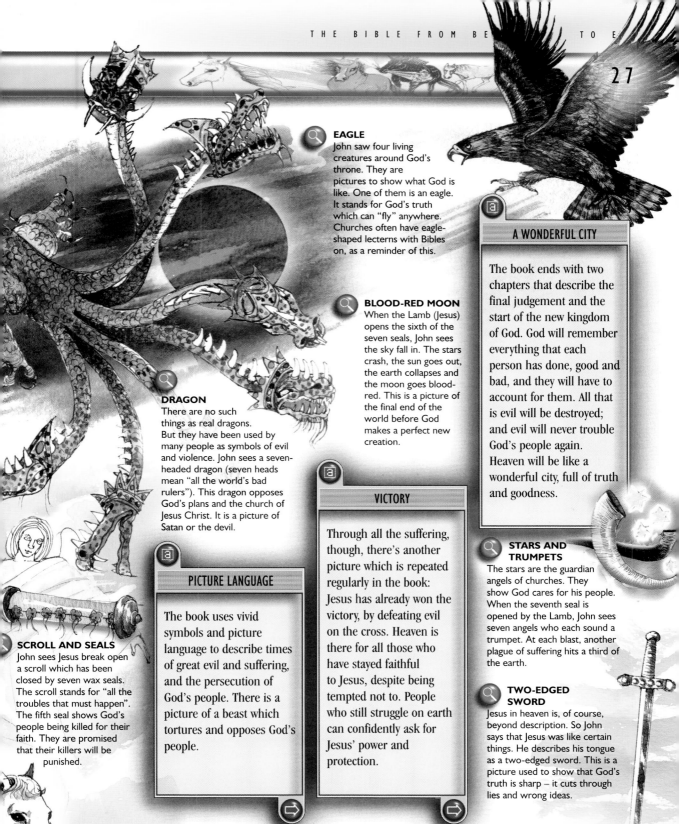

EAGLE
John saw four living creatures around God's throne. They are pictures to show what God is like. One of them is an eagle. It stands for God's truth which can "fly" anywhere. Churches often have eagle-shaped lecterns with Bibles on, as a reminder of this.

BLOOD-RED MOON
When the Lamb (Jesus) opens the sixth of the seven seals, John sees the sky fall in. The stars crash, the sun goes out, the earth collapses and the moon goes blood-red. This is a picture of the final end of the world before God makes a perfect new creation.

DRAGON
There are no such things as real dragons. But they have been used by many people as symbols of evil and violence. John sees a seven-headed dragon (seven heads mean "all the world's bad rulers"). This dragon opposes God's plans and the church of Jesus Christ. It is a picture of Satan or the devil.

A WONDERFUL CITY
The book ends with two chapters that describe the final judgement and the start of the new kingdom of God. God will remember everything that each person has done, good and bad, and they will have to account for them. All that is evil will be destroyed; and evil will never trouble God's people again. Heaven will be like a wonderful city, full of truth and goodness.

PICTURE LANGUAGE
The book uses vivid symbols and picture language to describe times of great evil and suffering, and the persecution of God's people. There is a picture of a beast which tortures and opposes God's people.

VICTORY
Through all the suffering, though, there's another picture which is repeated regularly in the book: Jesus has already won the victory, by defeating evil on the cross. Heaven is there for all those who have stayed faithful to Jesus, despite being tempted not to. People who still struggle on earth can confidently ask for Jesus' power and protection.

STARS AND TRUMPETS
The stars are the guardian angels of churches. They show God cares for his people. When the seventh seal is opened by the Lamb, John sees seven angels who each sound a trumpet. At each blast, another plague of suffering hits a third of the earth.

TWO-EDGED SWORD
Jesus in heaven is, of course, beyond description. So John says that Jesus was like certain things. He describes his tongue as a two-edged sword. This is a picture used to show that God's truth is sharp – it cuts through lies and wrong ideas.

SCROLL AND SEALS
John sees Jesus break open a scroll which has been closed by seven wax seals. The scroll stands for "all the troubles that must happen". The fifth seal shows God's people being killed for their faith. They are promised that their killers will be punished.

750 BC   500 BC   250 BC   AD 50–90

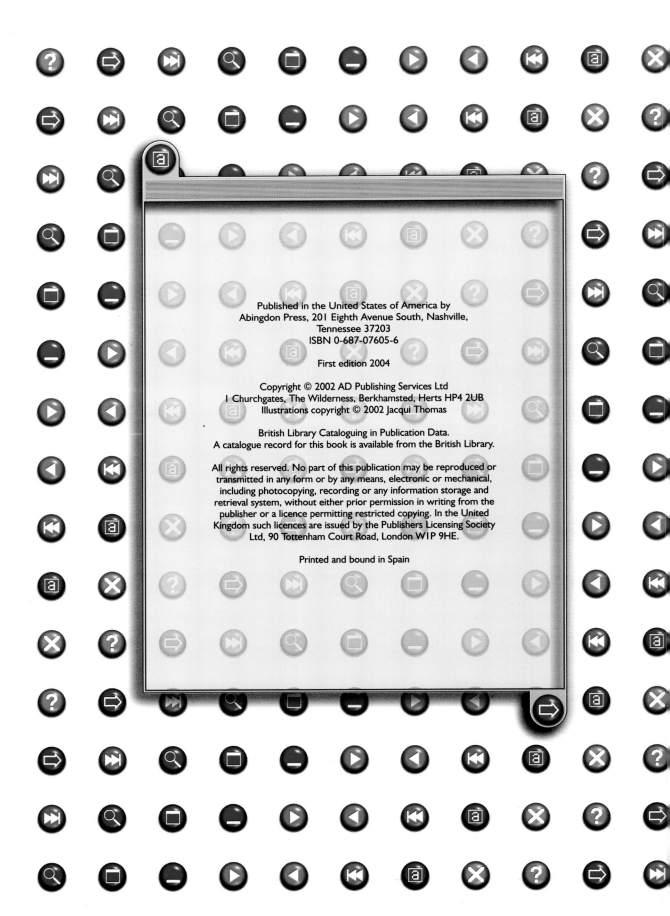

Published in the United States of America by
Abingdon Press, 201 Eighth Avenue South, Nashville,
Tennessee 37203
ISBN 0-687-07605-6

First edition 2004

Copyright © 2002 AD Publishing Services Ltd
1 Churchgates, The Wilderness, Berkhamsted, Herts HP4 2UB
Illustrations copyright © 2002 Jacqui Thomas

British Library Cataloguing in Publication Data.
A catalogue record for this book is available from the British Library.

Printed and bound in Spain